Exploring the Library

BY ALICE K. FLANAGAN

CONTENT ADVISERS: Carole Fiore, M.S. in L.S., Youth Services Consultant, Florida Department of State, Division of Library and Information Services, and Vice President and President-elect, Association for Library Service to Children; and Helen Rosenberg, M.L.S., Chicago Public Library

Gareth Stevens Publishing
A WORLD ALMANAC EDUCATION GROUP COMPANY

We would like to thank the staff of the following libraries for assisting us in the production of this book.

Algonquin Public Library

Channing Memorial School

Chicago National College of Naprapathy

Chicago Public Library— Edgebrook Branch

Chicago Public Library— Near North Branch

Dominican University Library

Evanston Public Library

Fremont Public Library

John Middleton School

Loyola University School of Law Library

Niles Public Library

Park Ridge Public Library

Please visit our web site at: **www.garethstevens.com**
For a free color catalog describing Gareth Stevens' list of high-quality books and multimedia programs, call 1-800-542-2595 (USA) or 1-800-461-9120 (Canada). Gareth Stevens Publishing's Fax: (414) 332-3567.

Library of Congress Cataloging-in-Publication Data

Flanagan, Alice K.
    Exploring the library / by Alice K. Flanagan.
       p. cm.
    Includes bibliographical references and index.
    Summary: Examines libraries and the many resources they have to offer — print, audiovisual, and online — and explains how to use them.
       ISBN 0-8368-2955-7 (lib. bdg.)   ISBN 0-8368-3014-8 (softcover)
       1. Libraries—Juvenile literature.   [1. Libraries.] I. Title.
Z665.5.F55   2001
027—dc21   2001034179

This North American edition first published in 2001 by
Gareth Stevens Publishing
A World Almanac Education Group Company
330 West Olive Street, Suite 100
Milwaukee, WI 53212 USA

This edition © 2001 by Gareth Stevens Publishing.

All photographs © World Almanac Education Group.

An Editorial Directions book
Editors: E. Russell Primm, M.A., University of Chicago, Graduate Library School; Emily Dolbear
Copy Editor: Irene Keller
Proofreader: Lucia Raatma
Indexer: Timothy J. Griffin
Designer: The Design Lab
Photographs by Romie Flanagan, Flanagan Publishing Services

Printed in the United States of America

1 2 3 4 5 6 7 8 9 05 04 03 02 01

Table of Contents

Libraries Aren't Just Buildings Anymore

GO TO A LIBRARY, and you can take a trip to Mars or scan the ocean floor. With the turn of a page, you can meet the most fascinating people. Some lived in the distant past, and some walk the Earth today. In the time it takes to click a mouse, you can travel around the world. Go to a library, and you can read about the best MP3 player or borrow sheet music for a school play.

In a library, you can learn about the present, investigate the past, and plan for the future. Most important, you can do all of this in one place.

But a library is more than a building. A library is a collection of information sources. A library is much more than you probably imagined. It isn't just a place to do your homework or find a fact. A library is an adventure.

Computers are an important part of modern libraries.

CHAPTER ONE

What Kinds of Libraries Are There?

LIBRARIES ARE EVERYWHERE. Some are on wheels. Some float. Some are behind prison bars. Some are on college campuses. Some are in the offices where people work. You may even have a library in your own home. Do you have books on a bookshelf? That's a library! Some libraries have no shelves at all. They are completely **electronic**. The one thing all libraries have in common is that they exist to serve people. (These people are called **patrons**.)

Public Libraries

The libraries people are most familiar with are public libraries. Most cities and towns in the United States and Canada have public libraries. They are open to everyone, free of charge.

It costs lots of money to keep libraries

Books are just a part of the many kinds of materials you can explore at the library.

5

THE TEN LARGEST U.S. PUBLIC LIBRARIES

Institution	Volumes
New York Public Library (Manhattan, Staten Island, and the Bronx boroughs of New York City)	10,421,691
Public Library of Cincinnati and Hamilton County (Ohio)	9,608,333
Chicago Public Library (Illinois)	9,238,328
Queens Borough Public Library (Queens borough of New York City)	9,143,760
The Free Library of Philadelphia (Pennsylvania)	8,144,478
Boston Public Library (Massachusetts)	7,438,880
County of Los Angeles Public Library (California)	7,289,562
Brooklyn Public Library (Brooklyn borough of New York City)	6,809,959
Carnegie Library of Pittsburgh (Pennsylvania)	6,303,408
Los Angeles Public Library (California)	5,722,733

U.S. PUBLIC LIBRARIES

Central buildings	8,943
Branches	7,147
Total buildings	16,090

CANADIAN PUBLIC LIBRARIES

Central buildings (including branches)	3,101

open and stocked with materials, however. Most of the money that pays for public libraries comes from the taxes people pay. The rest of the money comes from book sales, donations, and contributions from organizations such as Friends of the Library.

Public libraries are designed to serve their communities. For example, a public library in a large city provides materials in many languages. A library in a farming town may have lots of books on agriculture or information on 4-H projects. In Berkeley, California, the public library system runs the Berkeley Tool Library, where patrons can borrow tools!

Libraries in large communities may have many **branches.** Smaller towns and cities often have all the library materials under one roof.

Some public libraries have **bookmobiles.** These traveling libraries bring books and other materials to people who may be unable to visit the main library. The first bookmobile was a horse-drawn wagon that carried books in Maryland in 1905! These days, a bookmobile might stop near a park to bring picture books, video-tapes, and games to children or visit a retirement center to bring **large-print books** and sound recordings to seniors.

Bookmobiles stop at various sites each day for one or two hours.

One of the Chicago Public Library's bookmobiles

You can call your local library to find out when and where a bookmobile will be in your area.

School Libraries

The United States has more school libraries than any other kind of library. Most schools have a library for students and teachers. Elementary, middle, junior high, and high school libraries provide general information on a wide range of subjects.

Many school libraries contain computers.

The purpose of school libraries is to support the **curriculum**—all the subjects you study in your classes. Here you'll find books for your research papers, a novel or **biography** to read for a book report, and a newspaper or magazine for learning about current events.

Many school libraries also have books about subjects that are not included in the curriculum. You might find a novel by your favorite author, for example, or a book on judo, or a magazine with a tempting recipe.

Academic and Research Libraries

Libraries at colleges and universities are more extensive than public libraries or school libraries. They contain thousands or even millions of books, **periodicals,** and other materials. Academic libraries serve a community of students and professors. But people not con-

U.S. SCHOOL LIBRARIES

Public schools 77,218
Private schools 20,951
Total 98,169

THE TEN LARGEST U.S. ACADEMIC LIBRARIES

Institution	Volumes
Harvard University	14,190,704
Yale University	10,294,792
University of Illinois–Urbana/Champaign	9,302,203
University of California–Berkeley	8,946,754
University of Texas–Austin	7,783,847
University of California Los Angeles	7,401,780
University of Michigan	7,195,097
Stanford University	7,151,546
Columbia University	7,144,703
Cornell University	6,448,496

nected to the academic institution are often allowed to use the library at a college or university.

Medical, law, and business schools have libraries too. These libraries help students, researchers, and professors keep up with the latest developments in their fields.

Historical societies also have libraries. They preserve information about their states, counties, cities, or towns. They offer census records, letters, artifacts, maps, and historical photographs for researchers, publishers, and interested members of the community.

Many cities have private research libraries that are not connected to any larger organization. For example, the Newberry Library in Chicago, Illinois, is an independent research library. Known for its extensive materials on the American West and family history, this private library has more than 1.5 million volumes and 5 million **manuscript** pages.

Academic libraries have very extensive collections that aid both students and scholars.

Special Libraries

Special libraries serve the people in large organizations. Law firms, automobile companies, advertising agencies, newspapers, religious institutions, book publishers, and zoos usually have special libraries.

Many museums have special libraries. Art museums, science museums, natural history museums, and children's museums all maintain their own libraries. They provide information about a specific area of knowledge. While these museum libraries exist to serve their museum workers, other people are often permitted to use them if they can show a need.

Even prisons and ships have special libraries! The Folsom State Prison Library in California, for example, lends books and newspapers to its inmates. During visiting hours, prisoners can read to their children. In the library aboard the U.S.S. *Abraham Lincoln,* the ship's crew can check out books and keep up with current events.

The Newberry Library is in Chicago.

U.S. ARMED FORCES AND GOVERNMENT LIBRARIES

In 2000, the U.S. armed forces operated 341 libraries. Various government agencies maintain a total of 1,411 libraries.

U.S. SPECIAL LIBRARIES

In 2000, the United States had almost 10,000 special libraries.

Presidential Libraries

Presidential libraries are another kind of U.S. library. These libraries collect and maintain the various materials from a person's presidency. There are twelve of these libraries. Each presidential library also has a museum that is open to the public.

National Libraries

The Library of Congress is the national library of the United States. The federal government founded this library for members of Congress in 1800. Over time, the library has taken on other important roles. Every day, it receives 22,000 new items and adds about 10,000 of them to its collections. Only half of the library's collection is in English.

The Internet and the Library

The Internet has forever changed the way people use libraries. The Internet allows people to access online information at the library. The Internet also allows people at home to connect to their public library's online catalog and databases. If you can't get to your local public library—or if you want to explore a public library thousands of miles away—the Internet will take you there!

The Internet is a network of millions of computers around the world. The most famous part of the Internet is the World Wide Web. The World Wide Web—the graphical part of the Internet—is accessed through pages of linked text.

There are tens of millions of Web sites. Many are free, while some provide service for a fee. Some Web sites can only be used in a library. A **virtual library** is a Web site with some of the same reference information—or links to information—as a traditional library. No matter how you use the Internet, it has become a valuable tool for anyone with a computer.

Home Libraries

Many people have small libraries at home. Many home libraries start out small with books that parents buy to read with their children. Later, children need books to help them with their

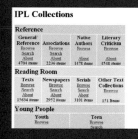

homework. Before long, families have a mini-library of books that inform and entertain. Sometimes favorite books remain with a family for generations.

Some people enjoy building a personal library as a hobby. These people are called **bibliophiles.** They collect books just as others may collect Pokémon cards or **CDs** (compact discs). Some bibliophiles have libraries so large that they have to construct a building just for their books!

Do you have a few favorite books at home? Then you have the beginnings of a library. If you expand your collection and keep it in good order, you might create a library that others can use. In 1815, Thomas Jefferson sold his personal collection to the young United States. It became the core of the Library of Congress after the British destroyed the original library collection during the War of 1812.

above: Children use a computer to look up information.
below: Favorite books can be read over and over again!

CHAPTER TWO

What's in a Library?

LIBRARIES PROVIDE a variety of resources to help you learn. You can read, view, or listen to information at a library. Books, videotapes, computer games, electronic databases, and even helpful people can be found in a library. **Audiovisual** materials such as videotapes, filmstrips, cassette tapes, CDs, **DVDs** (digital versatile discs), and **CD-ROMs** (compact discs read-only memory) are also very common. Of course, most libraries also have books, magazines, and newspapers.

A librarian helps find a book in a library.

Books

Books are one of the main resources in a library. People often think of books as falling into two categories: **fiction** and **nonfiction.** Most storybooks, picture books, folktales, fairy tales, poetry, plays, and novels are fiction. They are usually invented tales about imaginary characters and events. Nonfiction

13

Display racks make popular books more easily accessible.

books provide information about real people and events. Biographies, **auto-biographies,** essays, history books, and diaries are examples of nonfiction.

Look for the fiction and nonfiction sections in your library. Libraries often have signs pointing out these areas. Fiction titles are arranged in alphabetical order according to the author's last name. Nonfiction books are grouped by subject, according to the **Dewey decimal classification (DDS) system** or the **Library of Congress (LC) classification system**. Each book has a **call number** to help you find it. (See pages 31–35 for more information.)

Periodicals

Periodicals are publications published at specified intervals. Newspapers, magazines, and **journals** are types of periodicals. Newspapers are usually published daily, weekly, or monthly. Magazines are usually published weekly or monthly. Some journals are published only a few times a year!

Your library should have a list of the hundreds of periodicals to which it subscribes. To help you find information in magazines, you can use an **index** called *The Readers' Guide to Periodical Literature.* Some libraries may have a *Readers' Guide for Young People* on

WHERE IS IT SHELVED?	TITLE	AUTHOR	TYPE OF BOOK	CALL NUMBER
	The American Revolution	Bonnie Lukes	Nonfiction	973.3 Lukes. B.
	Laura Ingalls Wilder: A Biography	William Anderson	Biography	Biog. Wilde. L. Ander.W
	Little House on the Prairie	Laura Ingalls Wilder	Fiction	FIC*
	On the Way Home	Laura Ingalls Wilder	Autobiography	Biog. Wilde. L. Wilde. L

Shelved in the fiction section under "Wilder"

Libraries subscribe to many newspapers, such as the New York Times.

CD-ROM. Ask a librarian to help you find and use this resource in book form or on the computer.

Go to the index and select your topic. The index will list the magazines and newspapers that have published related articles. If the articles are recent, you might be able to read them from the printed magazine or newspaper. Some might be available online. You may have to use a special machine to read some articles. Older articles may be available on a CD-ROM.

Some electronic indexes provide more than just references to the information you are looking for. They also include the full texts of the articles. Among the most popular ones are ProQuest, FirstSearch, EBSCO Host, and Electric Library.

E-Books

Today, some library collections include electronic books called **E-books.** Some E-books are on CD-ROM. When you put the CD into a computer, you can read the complete works of authors such as Mark Twain or Beatrix Potter. Other E-books can be downloaded from the Internet in simple text formats that you can read on a word-processing program.

Today, easy-to-read electronic books are available for palm-

SOME IMPORTANT DAILY U.S. NEWSPAPERS

The New York Times
The Chicago Tribune
The Los Angeles Times
The Miami Herald
The Washington Post

SOME POPULAR MAGAZINES FOR YOUNGER READERS

Highlights for Children
National Geographic World
Muse
Odyssey: Adventures in Science
Time for Kids
Teen Newsweek
Teen
Sports Illustrated for Kids
U.S. Kids
YM

SOME SPECIALTY NEWSPAPERS

Daily Variety
Financial Times
The Hollywood Reporter
Investor's Daily
The Wall Street Journal

Some books are also
published as E-books.

size computers or pocket PC's. Libraries can purchase this software for use in these handheld, wireless computers. *Alice in Wonderland* and *The Wizard of Oz* are a few of the many children's books available in this format.

You need special software to use some E-books. Rocket e Book and SoftBook are two companies that have developed special hardware and software for reading electronic books. Microsoft has also developed a special type format that allows users to read electronic text more easily on both desktop and laptop computers, as well as on handheld personal computers.

Reference Books

To many people, reference books are the most important part of a library. These books represent some of the most-used materials in the library. Although many reference books are available in electronic form, patrons still rely on the book form. **Encyclopedias,** dictionaries and **thesauruses, atlases** and **gazetteers, almanacs** and **fact books,** and field guides are some of the many reference materials you'll find at the library.

Columbia Encyclopedia, print and online at *http://www.bartleby.com65/*

Merriam-Webster Collegiate Encyclopedia, print only

Americana, print and online at *http://go.grolier.com* (subscription only)

Collier's Encyclopedia, CD-ROM

Comptons, print and online at *http://www.comptons.com*

Encarta, CD-ROM and online at *http://www.encarta.msn.com* (selected information free, subscription only for whole database)

Encyclopaedia Britannica, print, CD-ROM, and online at *http://www.britannica.com*

Funk & Wagnalls, online only at *http://www.funkandwagnalls.com*

Grolier Encyclopedia, CD-ROM only

The New Book of Knowledge, print and online at *http://go.grolier.com* (subscription only)

New Standard, print only

World Book, print, CD-ROM, and online at *http://www.worldbookonline.com* (subscription only)

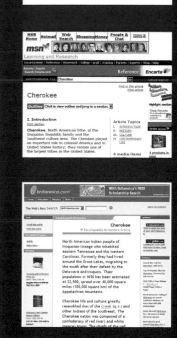

Encyclopedias

Encyclopedias provide information on many topics which are subjects arranged in alphabetical order. The two types of encyclopedias are general and special. General encyclopedias include articles on almost any topic you can think of.

Special encyclopedias provide information on specific subjects. These encyclopedias number in the thousands and cover topics ranging from careers to computers, mammals to medicine, and history to horticulture.

Multivolume encyclopedias are made up of several volumes. Each book has its own number or letter of the alphabet printed on its spine. Thus, the set is easily kept together in alphabetical or numerical order on the shelves. Your school or public library probably has more than one encyclopedia in its collection. Look for them in book form on the library shelves or in CD-ROM form.

Encyclopedias are often published in many volumes.

You can use some encyclopedias electronically on your computer through CD-ROMS or DVDs or on the Internet. Some electronic encyclopedias are combined with other reference materials to create reference suites. These materials often include other encyclopedias, dictionaries, atlases, and almanacs.

Dictionaries and Thesauruses

A dictionary lists words in alphabetical order and provides information about each word. You can learn the meaning of the word, its origins, and when it was first used. A dictionary also tells you how to pronounce the word. Some dictionaries have illustrations.

Many kinds of dictionaries are available today. They include picture dictionaries, children's dictionaries, computer dictionaries, and foreign-language dictionaries. There are special dictionaries too. Biographical dictionaries profile famous people in many fields, countries, or time periods. Some dictionaries provide historical facts about the United States or other countries of the world. Even sign language dictionaries are found in libraries today.

Shelved near the dictionaries are thesauruses. A thesaurus is a

Dictionaries help with more than just the meanings of words.

listing of words with their synonyms (words with the same or nearly the same meaning). Students often rely on a thesaurus when they are writing. *Roget's 21st Century Thesaurus* is a popular thesaurus.

Atlases and Gazeteers

An atlas is a book of maps. An atlas may feature road maps, maps that show specific countries and states, weather maps, population maps, illustrated maps, or historical maps. The historical *Atlas of the North American Indian* shows you where major North American Indian tribes lived throughout history. You can find all kinds of atlases in a library, including atlases for small towns, atlases for the

Atlases contain many kinds of information about places around the world.

world, and even space atlases!

A gazetteer provides population figures and other basic facts for cities, towns, and regions of the world. It also provides information about flags. Many gazetteers also have Web sites.

Almanacs and Fact Books

Almanacs provide facts at a glance. They answer questions such as: What is the tallest building in the world? What are the three largest cities in the United States? (In case you're wondering, Petronas Towers in Kuala Lumpur, Malaysia, are the tallest buildings in the world at present, and New York City, Los Angeles, and Chicago are the three largest cities in the United States.)

Many different kinds of almanacs and fact books are available today. The World Factbook, published by the Central Intelligence Agency, has useful information about the nations of the world. Most fact books are updated each

ALMANACS AND FACT BOOKS

ESPN Information Please Sports Almanac

Guinness World Records (online at *http://www. guinnessworldrecords. com*)

The New York Times Almanac

The Old Farmers Almanac (online at *http://www.almanac.com*)

Sports Illustrated Sports Almanac

Statesman's Yearbook

Time Almanac: With Information Please (online at *http://www. infoplease.com*)

The World Almanac and Book of Facts (online at *http://www.facts.com* subscription only)

The World Almanac for Kids

The World Fact Book (online at *http://www.odci. gov/cia/publications/ factbook* or *http://www. bartleby.com/151*)

year. Ask your librarian to show you an almanac or fact book just for kids!

Field Guides

Field guides are reference books about nature. They help you observe nature in the field. Field guides are filled with pictures, charts, illustrations, and useful terms. These books tell you all about insects, flowers, rocks and minerals, and even snakes.

Almanacs are filled with fascinating facts and information.

Other Reference Books

Your library has lots of other reference materials, of course. You can find famous sayings in *Bartlett's Familiar Quotations,* guidelines for writers and editors in *The Chicago Manual of Style,* telephone numbers in various directories, family histories in genealogy volumes, and population counts in *Statistical Abstract of the United States: The National Data Book* as well as other government manuals.

Online Resources

Many wonderful online resources are available to you at most libraries. You can use several search engines to look for information on the Internet. A search engine is a Web site that contains a database that indexes Web sites and Web pages. You type in **key words** to begin your search. The Internet has dozens of search engines.

OUT IN THE FIELD

Harper and Row's Complete Field Guide to North American Wildlife

National Audubon Society Field Guide to North American Butterflies

National Geographic's Guide to Wildlife Watching

Peterson's Guide to Western Birds

Simon and Schuster's Guide to Insects

SOME OTHER REFERENCE BOOKS

American Indian Myths and Legends

Bartlett's Familiar Quotations (online at http://www.bartleby.com/100)

Chronicle of the 20th Century

Facts and Dates in American Sports

Grangers Index to Poetry

SOME INTERNET SEARCH ENGINES

AskJeeves
http://www.askjeeves.com

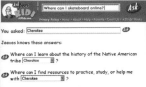

Ask Jeeves for Kids
http://www.ajkids.com

Excite
http://www.excite.com

Google
http://www.google.com

Hotbot
http://www.hotbot.lycos.com

Yahooligans
http://www.yahooligans.com

Some are general and others are specialized to index specific subjects and topics. Remember, however, that just as with printed and broadcast information, Web sites found through search engines can be unreliable or inaccurate.

When you are online, you can get help with homework. You can find information in many forms, including words, pictures, sound, and video. You can search books, newspapers, magazines, pictures, maps, or TV and radio. You can even print out the answers to your research questions on a printer, if your library has one.

Search engines on the Internet make finding information easy.

CHAPTER THREE

Mapping out the Library

A LIBRARY HAS SEVERAL SPECIAL AREAS. Each section has its own purpose and specially trained professionals and clerks. The areas you will probably use most often are the lending areas, the periodicals area, and the reference area.

The lending areas have all the items that can be borrowed for a specified amount of time (usually from one to three weeks). That includes hardcover and paperback books, videos, audiocassettes, and CD-ROMs. In this part of a library, you will find a **library catalog** of all the materials in the library. The lending areas include the adult, children's, and audiovisual and **multimedia** sections.

Using the library catalog helps to find items in the library's collection.

Adult Section

The adult section has books for older readers. It is usually divided into fiction and nonfiction. Many libraries have a separate area for biographies. Fiction is shelved alphabetically by the author's last name. Nonfiction is shelved using the DDS or LC classification systems (see pages 31–35 for more information).

Children's Section

Almost every public library has a children's section. Some libraries call it the "juvenile" or "family" section. Here, children's materials are kept on shelves that kids can easily reach. Librarians try to make this area as inviting to young people as possible.

This part of the library has books, videos, audiotapes, DVDs, CDs, games, puzzles, and periodicals especially for young people. Books in this section include **board books,** picture books, easy readers, and chapter books, to name just a few.

The fiction section, which consists mostly of novels, is shelved in alphabetical order according to the author's last name. Nonfiction (or information) books are usually grouped by subject. Each book has a set of numbers and letters on its spine to tell you where it belongs. The letters JUV (Juvenile), YP (Young Person), YA (Young Adult), or E (Easy) let you know that the book is intended for young people.

Books are often shelved according to reading difficulty or type. Many children's areas have special racks for the most popular books and subjects.

Some libraries are beginning to develop Young Adult sections

Libraries usually have entire sections for children's books.

Young adult books are sometimes shelved in their own area.

Computers in the library can also be used for music and games!

for older readers. In these areas, young people can find the materials they need without having to go to the adult section.

Audiovisual and Multimedia Area

The audiovisual and multimedia section of a library is a popular area. Some libraries provide listening and viewing stations. Here you can listen to music cassettes and CDs, books on tape, and foreign-language tapes. You might also be able to play educational computer games or try out new software programs. In some libraries, you can borrow movies on videocassette or DVD.

Periodicals Area

In this part of the library, you'll find patrons sitting in comfortable chairs reading *YM* magazine, *The Economist*, or a local newspaper. The area has magazines, newspapers, and journals on many subjects for a variety of readers. The periodicals area is intended to provide both entertainment and information.

Display racks hold the current issue of each periodical with a few **back issues** stacked behind it or on a rack below. Some libraries

SOME CD-ROM GAMES

The Amazing Writing Machine

Backyard Baseball

Jump Start

Math Blaster

Oregon Trail

Libraries subscribe to periodicals that appeal to many different interests.

circulate the back issues. Periodicals from past years are kept on **microfilm** or **microfiche,** so you may have to go to the reference area to look at those. Online periodical databases are also available.

Reference Area

The reference area is a very busy place indeed. The phone is constantly ringing with calls from patrons with questions. Other patrons are using online catalogs, reading at desks, and making inter-library loan (ILL) requests. A young woman might be researching her family history using microfilm of census records or reviewing Small Business Administration (SBA) pamphlets from the **vertical file.** (A vertical file is made up of one or more filing cabinets stocked with unbound materials, such as drawings, maps, and other materials difficult to keep on a shelf.) A retired person might be reading *Value Line's Investment Survey* and annual reports from corporations, or a young boy might be researching the value of his baseball card and Hot Wheels collections. All of these activities make the reference area a very busy place.

The heart of the reference area, however, is the reference desk.

The reference librarians are trained to help patrons find the answers they need. These librarians surround themselves with ready reference materials. These are books and online sources to help them answer the most commonly asked questions.

Librarians are ready to help patrons find what they need.

Materials in the reference area are called **noncirculating items.** These materials can't be checked out. They are kept in the library so that patrons and librarians always have access to them. They include encyclopedias, almanacs, atlases, and dictionaries of all kinds. Many libraries put the letters "REF" on the spine of reference books to tell you that they cannot be taken out of the library.

Many public libraries offer Internet access terminals. They may be located in the reference section of the library or in their own special area. Ask the reference librarian where they are in your library.

Viewing a special exhibit at the library

Other Areas

Many public libraries have exhibits that change regularly. They display items from their own collections or another library collection or even items from community members. Exhibits might include local historical photographs or artifacts. A special exhibit in the children's section might have an iguana or a tank full of exotic fish.

Libraries may also offer quiet reading rooms, meeting rooms for local organizations, study centers for young adults, or a storytelling room for children. Some libraries even have small auditoriums for film screenings, guest speakers, and live performances. Have you been to the library lately? It's not the place you think it is!

Behind the Scenes

Behind the scenes, librarians and clerks keep the library running. Librarians do many things that you might not know about. For example, librarians catalog, order, and manage their collection of materials. They are also responsible for the library's budget.

In a part of the library closed to the public, librarians decide which books to repair or rebind. They also decide which materials to remove permanently from the library. This process is called **weeding.** Librarians weed out materials that are no longer up-to-date. They also weed out materials damaged beyond repair and materials too fragile for the public to use. Librarians need to make space for new books, audiotapes, videotapes, CDs, and DVDs!

Special Services

Library patrons include people with disabilities. Most libraries offer special services to these people.

Some libraries, for example, have home service for people who are homebound. They also have services for patrons who are visually impaired or hearing impaired.

At many public libraries, visually impaired patrons have

A magnifier helps people who are visually impaired.

access to large-print books, magnifiers, and computers with large screens. In some libraries, a patron can listen through headphones to reading machines or computers that convert printed words into speech. Some visually impaired people read **braille** books. They read by moving their fingertips lightly across lines of raised dots. Each number and letter of the alphabet has its own pattern of dots.

For the hearing impaired, many libraries provide headphones that amplify speech on videos, audiocassettes, and computers. Some libraries also have videos with captions that describe the action. Upon request, some libraries will provide a librarian who knows American Sign Language (ASL). Ask your librarian about the special services your library offers.

Braille books let visually impaired people read by touch.

Circulation Desk

The first and last place you see in the library is probably the circulation desk. This is where you present your library card and check out the **circulating items** that you have chosen. You may have a pile of picture books for your sister or brother, books to help you with

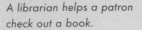
A librarian helps a patron check out a book.

a school project, a movie to watch with your friends, or a couple of best-sellers.

Today, libraries check out items in different ways. Some libraries use the pocket method. In this method, every circulating item has a paper pocket. In a library book, the pocket is usually on the first or last page. A librarian or **clerk** stamps the due date on a card and puts it in the pocket. The librarian scans the item's **bar code** and number into the computer. The bar code and number may be near the pocket. The librarian also scans your library-card number to keep a record of the books you check out. In addition, the librarian can also see if you have any books that have not been returned.

Some libraries no longer use the pocket method. Instead, they just scan the bar code and stamp a return date on the inside cover of the book. A few libraries are beginning to use another method. After they scan a bar code, they give a paper receipt to the borrower that shows when the book must be returned. Some libraries are experimenting with self-checkout terminals!

A machine scans the bar code in a book to check it out.

Many libraries have terminals for patrons to check out books themselves.

CHAPTER FOUR

Everything in Its Place

(AND HOW TO FIND IT)

*Looking at the flag
section of an almanac.*

LIBRARIES OFTEN HAVE THOUSANDS or even millions of items. How do librarians organize, store, and retrieve all those items? And how can you find what you are looking for at the library? Librarians could arrange the items by the physical size of the item or by publisher or by publication date. Over the years, however, librarians have developed classifications based on subject for the nonfiction materials. Fiction is usually arranged alphabetically by the author's last name.

Libraries in the United States, Canada, and other English-speaking countries often use one of two main classification systems. They are called the Dewey decimal classification (DDC) system and the Library of Congress (LC) classification system. In both systems, the library keeps a catalog that lists every item in its collection and each item has a call number. The call number helps you find the item on the shelves in the stacks.

31

A librarian can use a computer catalog to check up on library materials.

The Library Catalog

Librarians use the catalog to find items, monitor the collection, and check the dates when materials are due back. Patrons use the catalog to locate items of interest on the shelves. In the past, the catalog was kept on index cards in file drawers. A few libraries still use this **card catalog** method, but most school and public libraries now use **computer catalogs.**

You can search a library catalog in a number of ways. Author, title, and subject are the most common, but you can also search by series title, illustrator, or coauthor.

You will see the call number in the corner of the catalog card or on the computer screen. After you find your call number (and write it down!), follow signs to the row of shelves that contains your call number. Then you can **browse** through the stacks to find what you are looking for. If what you need isn't in your library, check with the reference librarian. It may be available from another library through inter-library loan.

Signs help this young patron find the book she's looking for.

The Dewey Decimal Classification (DDC) System

Most school and public libraries organize their books by the Dewey decimal classification (DDC) system. Melvil Dewey invented this system for small libraries in 1876. Under this system, books are divided into ten main groups or classes. Each class is identified by a set of numbers. Each class is then divided into ten subclasses. The original classification system was published in a forty-two page booklet. Today, it fills three volumes!

The Dewey decimal system includes a wide variety of subjects.

EXAMPLES OF CALL NUMBERS

The Adventures of Pinocchio, by Carlo Collodi	x398.4 Collo. C.*
Destination: Jupiter, by Seymour Simon	x523.45 Simon. S.
Famous Asian Americans (Collective biographies), by Janet Nomura Morey	x920 Morey
Favorite Greek Myths, by Mary Pope Osborne	x292 Osbor
Game Day: Behind the Scenes at a Ballpark, by Robert Young	x796.357 Young. R.
Gorillas, by Paul Fleisher	x599.884 Fleis
How We Choose a President, by Lee Learner Gray	x329 G 79h
Say Hola to Spanish, by Susan Middleton Elya	x463 Elya. S.
Shakespeare's Stories, by Leon Garfield	x822.33 Garfi. L.
Step-by-Step Cookbook, by Angela Wilke	x641.5 Wilke. A.
Voices from the Civil War, by Milton Meltzer	x973 Voices
A Weekend with Rembrandt, by Pascal Bonafoux	x759.9492 Rembran. Bonaf.
Where the Sidewalk Ends, by Shel Silverstein	x811 Silver. S.

*(x means juvenile)

THE DEWEY DECIMAL CLASSIFICATION SYSTEM

000 **General Knowledge (Almanacs, Encyclopedias, Libraries, Museums, Newspapers, etc.)**
010 Bibliographies
020 Library & Information Science
030 General Encyclopedias
040 (Not used)
050 General Periodicals
060 General Organizations & Museums
070 Journalism & Publishing
080 Collections
090 Manuscripts and Rare Books

100 **Psychology and Philosophy (Death & Dying, Ethics, Feelings, Logic, Making Friends, Optical Illusions, Superstitions)**
110 Metaphysics
120 Epistemology
130 Paranormal Phenomena & Occult
140 Specific philosophies
150 Psychology
160 Logic
170 Ethics
180 Ancient, Medieval & Oriental Philosophy
190 Modern Western Philosophy

200 **Religions and Mythology (Amish, Bible Stories, Christianity, Judaism, Islam, Quakers, Shakers)**
210 Natural Religion
220 Bible
230 Christian Theology
240 Christian Moral Theology
250 Local Church & Religious Orders
260 Social & Ecclesiastical Theology
270 History & Geography of Church
280 Christian Denominations & Sects
290 Non-Christian & Comparative Religion

300 **Social Sciences and Folklore (Careers, Customs, Environment, Families, Government, Manners, Money, Recycling)**
310 Statistics
320 Political Science
330 Economics
340 Law
350 Public Administration
360 Social Concerns & Services
370 Education
380 Trade & Commerce
390 Customs, Etiquette, Folklore

400 **Languages and Grammar (Chinese, English, French, German, Italian, Japanese, Sign Language, Spanish)**
410 Linguistics
420 English Language
430 Germanic & Scandinavian Languages
440 French
450 Italian
460 Spanish & Portuguese
470 Latin
480 Classical Greek
490 Other Languages

500 **Math and Science (Animals, Biology, Chemistry, Dinosaurs, Fish, Geology, Insects, Physics, Planets, Plants)**
510 Math
520 Astronomy
530 Physics
540 Chemistry
550 Earth Science
560 Paleontology
570 Life Sciences
580 Botany
590 Zoology

600 **Medicine and Technology (Computers, Engineering, Farming, Health, Human Body, Manufacturing, Nutrition)**
610 Medicine
620 Engineering
630 Agriculture
640 Home Economics
650 Management
660 Chemical Technologies
670 Manufacturing
680 Application-specific Manufacturing
690 Building

700 **Arts & Recreation (Architecture, Crafts, Drawing, Games, Jokes, Music, Puppets, Songbooks, Sports)**
710 Civic & Landscape Art
720 Architecture
730 Sculpture
740 Drawing
750 Painting
760 Graphic & Printed Art
770 Photography
780 Music
790 Sports & Recreation

800 **Literature (Children's Literature, Plays, Poetry, Shakespeare, Writing)**
810 American Literature
820 English Literature
830 Germanic Literature
840 French Literature
850 Italian Literature
860 Spanish & Portuguese Literature
870 Latin Literature
880 Classical Greek Literature
890 Literature of Other Languages

900 **Geography and History (Biographies, Countries, Native Americans, States, Travel, Wars)**
910 Travel & Geography
920 Genealogy & Geography
930 Ancient History
940 European History
950 Asian History
960 African History
970 North American History
980 South American History
990 History of Other Areas

Each of the subclassifications is further subdivided. Physics, for example, is subdivided as follows:
530 Physics
531 Solid mechanics
532 Fluid mechanics
533 Gas mechanics
534 Sound
535 Light
536 Heat
537 Electricity
538 Magnetism
539 Modern physics

With the use of a decimal point and extra digits after the point, each of these sections can be further subdivided to cover increasingly narrower subject areas.
For example, for Electricity
537.5 Electronics
537.534 Radio waves
537.5342 Long waves
537.5343 Short waves

The Library of Congress Classification System

Some large public libraries and many research libraries use the Library of Congress (LC) classification system. This system divides knowledge into twenty-one main classes. A single letter identifies each class. If you have trouble finding a call number, ask a librarian to help you.

Subject Headings

Many items in the library contain information about a number of subjects. This can make classifying the works difficult. The Dewey decimal classification system and the Library of Congress Classification system assign a work a single classification number. Because of this limitation, some of the work's topics may not be included. To help patrons locate materials more accurately, librarians assign a number of subject headings to each work. These headings may be a single word, many words, or even phrases that help describe the work's content. In the United States, two systems for creating subjects headings are used: the Library of Congress and the Sears List. The Library of Congress headings are used mainly by academic libraries, public libraries, and special libraries. School libraries often use the Sears List heading.

CHAPTER FIVE

Who Can Help You at the Library?

IF YOU NEED HELP at the library, many people can assist you. Perhaps the most important part of a librarian's job is helping the public use the library. The work of librarians and clerks is never done. They order materials, catalog books, and work at the circulation desk. They also organize exhibits and special library events. Before the end of the day, librarians in large libraries may have helped hundreds of patrons in person and on the phone.

At the Public Library

The public library may have several librarians and clerks to help you. They work as a team. Each person has a different job to do. Sometimes librarians take turns doing jobs. However, some public libraries have only one librarian to run the whole library. The following are a few of the many jobs librarians and clerks perform.

Librarians order new materials. Sometimes the head librarian is responsible for the ordering. Before librarians shelve materials,

36

Librarians work to help patrons use the library.

they give each item a classification number and list it in the library catalog. These librarians are called **catalogers.**

Librarians who specialize in finding information are called reference librarians. Most usually have a master's degree in **library science.** Some have other graduate degrees too. Reference librarians answer questions about almost anything. They help people use the catalog and find library materials and online information.

Librarians in the children's section of a library usually have one or more helpers. They are familiar with children's books, games, and other materials. A children's librarian can help you find a good book to read or use as research for school projects.

A cataloger applies a shelving label to the spine of a new book.

Librarians at the circulation desk of a library can be most helpful. Sometimes they check out hundreds of items a day. Each transaction is recorded in the computer—usually when the item is checked out and returned. After you return an item, it is put back on the shelves. During the busiest times of the day, several people may be working at the circulation desk.

The workers who return materials to the library shelves are called **shelvers** or **pages.** They carefully return each item to its proper place in the library so that patrons can find what they need.

HOW MANY PEOPLE WORK IN U.S. LIBRARIES?

	Librarians	Other Paid Staff	Total Staff
Academic Libraries	27,268	68,020	95,288
Public Libraries	27,946	92,804	120,750
School Libraries	72,160	92,483	164,643
Total	127,374	253,307	380,681*

*Figures for special libraries are not available, although the Special Library Association has 15,000 professional members who work in special libraries. The total number of people employed in special libraries is certainly higher.

One task for school librarians is reshelving materials.

Some libraries hire specialists to help their patrons. A specialist might take care of the library's audiovisual equipment. Other specialists might help patrons find information on the Internet. Librarians have to be informed about computers and software programs.

At the School Library

At the school library, librarians are sometimes called **media specialists.** They help the school's students and teachers. School libraries are not open to the general public. Sometimes, volunteers or part-time clerks help the librarians. In very small schools, the librarians might be volunteers.

School librarians have an enormous job. A typical day might include reading stories to the kindergarten children, setting up the computer lab for the fourth-grade classes, or teaching library skills to fifth-graders. Middle and high school librarians teach reference skills to help students do their schoolwork more efficiently.

Between group activities, school librarians are purchasing and cataloging new materials. They are checking out books, recording returns, and keeping the library in order. After school, many librarians put in extra time in the library decorating for holidays or working with teachers on classroom projects. Now and then, school librarians organize a special library event, such as a family reading night. Although school librarians are busy, they are there to help you learn more about the library and the world around you.

Helping students in a computer lab

CHAPTER SIX

What's Going on at the Library?

THERE'S MORE GOING ON at the library than research and reading. Libraries can be exciting places in many ways. Libraries can serve as community centers where the arts, education, and entertainment thrive.

The next time you're in a public library, ask the librarian about upcoming events. Or pick up one of their monthly activity calendars. Check to see if your library has its activity calendar online. Find out what's going on at your library!

Often local artists and photographers display their work at the library. Actors, musicians, and storytellers sometimes visit libraries to put on short performances or puppet shows. From time to time, authors and illustrators come to talk about their books and read from them. They might even sell copies of their books and autograph them. Libraries with auditoriums sometimes put on foreign-film programs.

An author talks to children about her book.

Libraries offer programs for everyone to participate in.

Throughout the year, many libraries offer literacy education, study classes, or holiday-craft programs. Most provide homework help for children and computer research online. Some libraries sponsor **book clubs.** The book club members meet at the library to discuss the books they have read.

Many public libraries organize summer reading programs for children. Some offer infant programs for babies and their parents. The program helps babies learn nursery rhymes and songs and enjoy visiting the library. One of the library's most popular events is story time, when the librarian reads stories to children.

Often, libraries have book fairs at which people buy books. They also hold job fairs to help people learn about new careers. Sometimes community groups hold meetings in the library. There's always something happening at the library!

The next time you go to a library, make it an adventure. Explore all the different areas. Observe what people are doing and how they are learning. Ask questions. Make at least one interesting discovery, and learn how to do one new thing. Then exploring the library will be fun.

CHAPTER SEVEN

Shhh! Quiet Please!

TIPS ON HOW TO BEHAVE AT THE LIBRARY

LIBRARIES ARE PLACES OF LEARNING. Here are some tips on the proper way to behave in a library.

- Be polite. Wait your turn for materials. If you have to wait for a librarian to help you, be patient. Remember to thank a librarian for his or her help.

- Share materials. Don't keep materials longer than necessary. You are not the only person who needs them.

- Help others. This makes using the library an enjoyable experience.

- Don't damage books or other materials. Remember, the library belongs to everyone.

- Keep your workplace clean. Pick up after yourself before you leave. Others have to use the space after you.

- Follow library rules and obey librarians. They are in charge of the library.

- Return all items to their proper place. Some libraries do not want you to return books and materials to the shelves. Look for signs that tell you where to leave the books that you don't want to check out.

41

A librarian shows a young patron how to use an online catalog.

Library Terms to Know

almanacs—books of general facts and statistics published once a year

atlases—books of maps

audiovisual—using sound and sight

autobiographies—books in which the writer tells the story of his or her own life

back issues—previous editions of a magazine

bar code—a band of lines containing information that can be read by a computer

bibliophiles—people who love books and reading

biography—a book that tells someone's life story

board books—picture books made of stiff paperboards

book clubs—groups whose members read books and meet to discuss them

bookmobiles—buses or vans used as traveling libraries

braille—a system of writing used for blind people. It uses raised dots that are felt by the fingertips.

branches—the neighborhood libraries that are part of a city's library system

browse—to look over casually in search of something of interest

call number—a combination of numbers that indicate where a book should be shelved in a library

card catalog—index cards that list all the library's materials

catalogers—librarians who give each item a classification number and list it in the library catalog

CDs (compact discs)—small plastic discs that store information and music digitally

CD-ROMs (compact discs read-only memory)—compact discs that produce words and pictures and is used on a computer

circulating items—items that can be checked out of a library

clerk—a library worker who assists professional librarians

computer catalog—a computer listing of all the materials a library owns

curriculum—a course of study

Dewey decimal classification (DDC) system—a method of organizing library materials that divides knowledge into ten main classes

DVDs (digital versatile discs)—a kind of digital storage system on plastic disks that holds more information than CD-ROMs

E-books—electronic books

electronic—powered by electricity

encyclopedias—books or sets of books containing information on many subjects and organized alphabetically

fact books—listings of information on general subjects

fiction—novels, picture books, poetry, plays, and writing about characters and events that are not real

gazetteers—geographical dictionaries

illuminated—decorated with designs, pictures, and bright colors

index—an alphabetical listing of the information in a book or other reference

journals—professional or academic periodicals

key words—words entered into a search engine to retrieve information on a particular subject

large-print books—books with print large enough for visually impaired people to read

library catalog—a listing of all a library's materials

Library of Congress (LC) classification system—a method of organizing library materials that divides knowledge into twenty-one main classes

library science—the study of library work

manuscript—an original written composition of something before it is published

media specialists—school librarian

microfiche—a sheet of film of printed pages

microfilm—a filmstrip of printed pages

multimedia—using various kinds of computer technologies such as video, sound, and text

noncirculating items—materials in the reference section of a library that cannot be checked out

nonfiction—writing that tells about real people, things, and events, such as biographies, autobiographies, essays, history books, and diaries

page proofs—early versions of the pages in a book before they are published

pages—library workers who shelve materials in the proper place; also called shelvers

patrons—people who use and support a library

periodicals—publications published at specified times

search engines—Internet software programs that help a person search for Web sites by using key words

shelvers—library workers who shelve materials in the proper place; also called pages

special libraries—libraries that serve members of large organizations

thesauruses—books of words followed by words with similar meanings

vertical file—one or more filing cabinets stocked with loose, unbound materials, such as drawings, maps, and other materials that are difficult to shelve

virtual library—a Web site with links to some of the same reference information as a traditional library

weeding—permanently removing items from a library collection

A Short History of Libraries

MORE THAN 30,000 YEARS AGO	Our ancestors paint pictures on the walls of caves to explain events. We might even say that these caves were the first libraries.
5000 B.C.	Egyptians record their history on a type of paper called papyrus. The papyrus sheets are rolled into long scrolls and kept in the Pharoahs' palaces, temples, and tombs.
ABOUT 3000 B.C.	The people of Mesopotamia (now Iraq) begin etching pictures on clay tablets to record special events, laws, and business transactions.
300s B.C.	The Greeks make libraries available to everyone. One of the most famous Greek libraries is in Alexandria, Egypt. It may have had more than 500,000 papyrus scrolls.
221–206 B.C.	The first libraries in China begin. The finest library belongs to the Emperor of China. It was called the Imperial Library.
200 B.C. TO A.D. 476	The Romans build many beautiful libraries.
1366	The first European national library is founded in Prague, in what is now the Czech Republic.
ABOUT 1450	The German inventor Johannes Gutenberg perfects a way to print books using a press and small pieces of metal type. His invention makes it possible to make multiple copies of a book.
LATE 1500s–EARLY 1600s	Europeans settle in North America and bring a few religious books with them, which they share with friends.
ABOUT 1638	A printing press is shipped from England to Cambridge, Massachusetts. Harvard College opens a library with 300 books. The Harvard Library is the first true library in the United States. Today, it holds more than 14 million books and is the oldest research library in the United States.
1731	Benjamin Franklin founds the Library Company of Philadelphia. It is the first society library in the United States. (A society library was made up of several people's personal libraries. To join a society library, people could buy shares. The money raised from the shares was then used to buy more books.)
1833	The oldest tax-supported public library in the United States begins in Peterborough, New Hampshire. The Peterborough Public Library is still open today.

1836	The U.S. government establishes the National Library of Medicine.
1848	The Boston Public Library is established and quickly becomes the model for other public libraries in the United States by allowing patrons to take books home.
1876	Melvil Dewey invents the Dewey decimal system for small libraries.
1886	The Library of Congress moves into its new home, the Thomas Jefferson Building.
EARLY 1900s	The Library of Congress begins developing its own classification system.
1938	The Library of Congress opens its second building—the John Adams Building.
1980	The third, and largest, of the Library of Congress's buildings opens—the James Madison Building.
1994	The U.S. government establishes the National Library of Education.
1997	The British Library moves into its new facility in the Saint Pancras section of London.
TODAY	The Library of Congress in Washington, D.C., is the world's largest library. Each day, it receives 22,000 new items and adds about 10,000 of them to the permanent collection. Today, the Library of Congress holds more than 100 million items.

Learning More about the Library

BOOKS

Appelt, Kathi. *Down Cut Shin Creek: The Packhorse Librarians of Kentucky.* New York: HarperCollins Children's Books, 2001.

Collins, Mary. *The Library of Congress.* Danbury, Conn.: Children's Press, 1998.

Gold, John Coppersmith. *Board of Education v. Pico: Book Banning.* New York: Twenty First Century Books, 1995.

Johnston, Marianne. *Let's Visit the Library.* New York: Rosen Publishing Group, 1999.

Simon, Charnan. *Andrew Carnegie: Builder of Libraries.* Danbury, Conn.: Children's Press, 1998.

Wu, Dana Ying-Hui. *Our Libraries.* Brookfield, Conn.: Millbrook Press, 2001.

WEB SITES

Library External Services—How to Use Libraries
http://wwwlib.murdoch.edu.au/services/external/extusinglibrary.html
To read online about how to use a library like the Murdoch Library

The Library of Congress
http://www.loc.gov
For information from the largest library in the world

Kids Connect: Ask KC
http://www.ala.org/ICONN/AskKC.html
For a site on which students can ask librarians questions

Rochester Middle School Media Center
http://www.rochesterschools.com/rms/library/library/html
To learn more about how to use the Dewey decimal system, the card catalog, and much more

PLACES TO WRITE

American Library Association
Public Information Office
50 East Huron Street
Chicago, IL 60611

Canadian Library Association
328 Frank Street
Ottawa, ON K2P 0X8 Canada

The Library of Congress
101 Independence Avenue, S.W.
Washington, DC 20540

PLACES TO VISIT

Berkeley Public Library
Tool Lending Library
1901 Russell Street
Berkeley, CA 94703

510/644-6101

To visit one of a few libraries in the United States to lend tools to its patrons

The J. Paul Getty Museum
1200 Getty Center Drive
Los Angeles, CA 90049

310/440-7300

To look at the large art collection, a reconstructed Roman villa, rotating exhibits as well as the research library devoted to art and architecture

John F. Kennedy Library and Museum
Columbia Point
Boston, MA 02125

877/616-4599

To see materials such as papers and tape recordings associated with John F. Kennedy's presidency as well as the Ernest Hemingway Collection, which contains papers and parts of famous manuscripts

The Library of Congress
101 Independence Avenue, S.E.
Washington, DC 20540

202/707-5000

To view the main Reading Room, Thomas Jefferson's Library, other exhibitions, and the "American Treasures" exhibit, which rotates 300 different pieces of American History such as James Madison's notes from the Constitutional Convention

The Morgan Library
29 East 36th Street
New York, NY 10016

212/685-0610

To view such important historical books as a copy of the Gutenberg Bible, ancient seals and tablets, **illuminated** manuscripts, and exhibits on art and literature

The New York Public Library
Humanities and Social Sciences Library
5th Avenue and 42nd Street
New York, NY 10018

To see the lions outside of one of the most famous public libraries in the United States as well as the rotating exhibitions on display inside

University of Chicago
1100 East 57th Street
Chicago, IL 60637

To visit the academic library at the University of Chicago, which houses a rare-book collection with more 255,000 volumes and manuscripts totaling 4,569 feet (1,394 meters), in addition to its academic collection

University of Minnesota Libraries
The Children's Literature Research Collection
113 Elmer L. Andersen Library
222 21st Avenue South
Minneapolis, MN 55455

612/624-4576

To view the Kerlan, Hess, Paul Bunyan, and Oz Collections, which feature a range of children's literature material from folklore about Paul Bunyan to figurines and comic books

Index

ABOUT THE AUTHOR

Alice K. Flanagan writes books for children and teachers. She has written more than seventy books. Some of her books include biographies of U.S. presidents and their wives, biographies of people working in our neighborhoods, phonics books for beginning readers, and informational books about birds and Native Americans. Alice K. Flanagan lives in Chicago, Illinois.